How Can Sign Chi Do Benefit My Health?

Medical studies show that wh suppressed for long periods of s, muscular tension, and poor po stress, the ability of the brain chemicals fail. This in turn ca cardiovascular system, it can v suppress the immune system, increase chances of diabetes, and put you at increased risk for developing ulcers.

Sign Chi Do was designed to facilitate the flow of your emotions so that they can be expressed in a creative, empowering way through your movements.

The word "emotion" is derived from the latin word "Emot", which means "outward moving" or "an outward expression of an inner feeling". The mind and body fitness phrases are built on this simple concept: that is, to outwardly express an inner feeling through the sign movements defining those words and emotions.

Now you may ask why sign language and not just arm movements? As far as the brain is concerned, plain arm gestures are not recognized in the language area of the brain. Sign language is processed in the language area of the brain because of the linguistic and communication properties it has. In sign chi do, the goal is to communicate in a way that will allow you to express your emotions through movement resulting in a calm, relaxed state. Sign language is perfect for that.

In conclusion, Sign Chi Do is a great way to live stress free—from the inside out!

SignChiDo
Dr. Anne Borik

SignChiDo Press
2023 W. Peninsula Circle
Chandler, AZ
(480) 628-EWAX
Website: www.SignChiDo.com

ISBN: 0-9755194-0-9
First printing

Editing: SageBrush Publications, Tempe, Arizona
Typesetting, Cover Design, Printing, Illustrations:
VAS Communications, Phoenix,Az
Photography: Jim Burk - VAS Communications, Phoenix,Az
Models:
Joe Borik
Dusty Vantilberg

Printed and bound in the United States of America

Acknowledgement

I want to thank my Heavenly Father for giving me the strength to complete this awesome project. I trust that He will continue to open the eyes of my heart to see and to do His will.

Thank you to my grandparents who have always been the role model of "Love" for me. May their souls rest in God's peace.

Thank you to my parents whose unconditional love and sacrifice I will never forget. I am grateful forever.

FOREWORD

Edward B. Diethrich, M.D.
Medical Director, Arizona Heart Institute

At a time when our nation is being threatened not by bombs and terrorists but rather by an epidemic of obesity, hypertension, diabetes mellitus, heart disease, and stroke, Dr. Anne Borik's: Sign Chi Do Mind and Body Fitness, is a refreshing contribution to an area of healthcare advisement that is all too often plagued by misconceptions, inaccurate information, and unproved hypotheses.

I personally know Anne and have worked closely with her in the care of our patients at the Arizona Heart Institute and Hospital. Her excitement about the project does not surprise me since she approaches every situation with vigor and enthusiasm. Her smile, friendliness, and outstanding patient relationships clearly reflects her own personal commitments to the concepts exposed in Sign Chi Do.

The principles of this program are both simple and already accepted by authorities in the field of good health and preventative medicine. We have long known that proper breathing is essential to our well-being and improper posture can be the route of many disorders. Just look around at your co-workers. No doubt those practicing proper breathing with good posture are the highest producers. Anne then stresses a third principle. The movements we make between postures - those transitional moves. Ever experience a pain in your back when you arise from a sitting to a standing position? And finally, we must all agree that feeling well can only occur when mind and body are in harmony. She introduces a new thought in chi flow, an energy source to enhance a feeling of good health. The book depicts this interesting process that could not be more profoundly illustrated than its exhilarating cover.

Above all, Dr. Borik has laid out, in both text and illustration, a clear description that enables everyone, in spite of age or current state of health, to initiate a program of better health and feeling well both in body and mind.

As she says: "Let's get started!"

ARIZONA HEART
INSTITUTE
2632 North 20th Street • Phoenix, Arizona 85006

About the Author

Dr. Anne Borik is an internal medicine physician who is also a third degree black belt. Anne started karate at the age of 8 and became a black belt by age 13. She has competed in many national and international competitions and was ranked 3rd in the world in the womens' black belt division in 1983. She went on to Temple University to study Exercise Physiology and got her medical degree from the Philadelphia College of Osteopathic medicine. Dr. Borik is board certified in Internal Medicine and is an adjunct assistant professor, division of clinical education at Midwestern University. She has pioneered the field of Hospitalists Medicine and currently is practicing as a hospitalist in Phoenix, Arizona. She has received many outstanding awards, including being voted as one of the Top Doctors in the Valley by Phoenix Magazine in 2000.

Dr. Borik has designed a new relaxation, exercise system called Sign Chi Do. It harmonizes the universal language of sign with movement and breathing resulting in "moving language". Sign Chi Do got its name by using the word "sign" which represents the universal language of sign. "Chi" is a word that defines the body's inner energy and "Do" means "the way". It also stands for Doctor of Osteopathic Medicine, which is what she is. Sign Chi Do is a unique exercise form whose essence is derived from the medical perspective and background knowledge of Dr. Anne Borik.

SIGN CHI DŌ
Table of Contents

Chapter 1

An Introduction to Sign Chi Do

S ignChiDo is an exercise form created and designed by a medical physician. It is intended to harmonize the universal language of sign with movement resulting in "moving language." It is not necessary to know sign language in order to practice SignChiDo. This book will take you step by step through the postures and sign techniques that depict the different words and phrases.

There are four groups of words. The first group are the introductory words. Second is the action stack of words including empowering and rejuvenating action words. Third are the "emotion" words, including warm and cool emotions. Last are the closing words. Once the collection of word techniques is learned, you will be able to combine the moving words into personalized statements. For example, "Be sincere to take on love, peace, and contentment forever," or "Be motivated to overcome depression and anxiety with confidence."

SignChiDo differs from other forms of exercise meditation in that thinking about the word movements that are being performed constantly stimulates the mind. This cognitive function, when combined with changing movements, has been found to enhance memory, concentration, and spiritual awareness and create an overall sense of well-being. Instead of emptying your mind, in SignChiDo you are encouraged to fill your mind with creative, powerful words that ultimately you communicate through your movements. By integrating the concepts of diaphragmatic breathing and chi flow with this movement, you will be able to attain a true state of relaxation.

Ultimately, SignChiDo is an excellent tool for stress reduction. When the body is under stress, whether it be mental stress or physical stress, the body releases certain chemicals into the blood called catecholamines. These chemicals cause increased blood pressure, increased heart rate, increased blood sugar, decreased or slow digestion, and over time, decreased circulation due to constriction of the blood vessels. SignChiDo was designed to combat stress by decreasing the release of those chemicals resulting in improved blood pressure, heart rate, blood sugar (especially in diabetics), and overall improved circulation.

SignChiDo is intended for people of all ages regardless of their physical abilities. It can be practiced anywhere since no special equipment is needed. This makes SignChiDo a great tool to help deal with stress on a daily basis. Because there are no limitations in how it is practiced, SignChiDo can be modified to be done in a chair, at a desk, or even in a bed.

Four basic principles form the foundation on which SignChiDo is built. First, **proper diaphragmatic breathing** is vital to the practice of SignChiDo. As a physician, I will outline the many benefits that proper breathing has on the body as it pertains to stress reduction, enhanced concentration, improved circulation, and more efficient digestion of food. The second principle is **posture**. This refers to the individual stance with specific hand sign movements representing each word or phrase. Proper alignment of the body is important in order to strengthen the muscles as well as prevent injury. The third principle is **transitional moves**. This refers to the movement between postures. Changing from one stance to another is transitional movement. Diaphragmatic breathing plays a very important role in the transitional moves. Properly used, these principles enable the continuity of movement to string multiple words together, resulting in an expressive statement using the entire body. The fourth principle is **chi flow**. This is the energy flow that results when the mind and body are in harmony.

Energy can be a confusing word. Energy is what creates an electrical impulse that causes the human heart to beat. As a result of the heart beating, blood is pumped out to feed the rest of the body. As this blood flows in the vessels, along with it flows a certain amount of that electrical impulse or "energy." It is this energy that we refer to as "chi." In this book, I will outline how chi flows through the body and how to tap into that energy source as a means of enhancing your overall state of health.

From a medical perspective, SignChiDo has beneficial effects on the different systems of the body including the digestive system, circulatory system, endocrine system, and cardiovascular system. I will specifically outline how SignChiDo can lower blood pressure, decrease risk for heart disease, reduce irritable bowel symptoms, enhance memory by increasing blood flow to the brain, decrease risk for diabetes, and improve fibromyalgia/chronic fatigue symptoms.

SignChiDo can be practiced any time of the day. You don't need a lot of space, and no specific dress code is required. As long as you are comfortable and your movements are not restricted, you should be able to practice SignChiDo. So let's get started!

Chapter 2

Diaphragmatic Breathing

Diaphragmatic Breathing

How To?

Diaphragmatic breathing, also called "belly breathing," is the type of breathing that we will practice in SignChiDo. It is the most efficient way to breathe. In order to learn this type of breathing, it is important to have a basic understanding of what the diaphragm is and how it functions in relationship to the lungs.

The diaphragm is a flat muscle that separates the chest from the lower abdominal cavity. The lungs, which fill up a large portion of the chest, rests above the diaphragm. All the abdominal organs are just below the diaphragm, including the intestines.

Now, imagine the diaphragm moving as you breathe. It moves downward as you breathe in, and moves up as you breathe out.

Before you read any further, STOP and feel your own breath. As you breathe in, imagine the diaphragm moving down, causing your belly to protrude. As you breathe out, the diaphragm moves up to its original position, and your belly moves inward.

The motion of the diaphragm as you breathe affects the abdominal organs such as the stomach and intestines. With each breath, the diaphragm moves down, causing the intestines to contract, which results in more efficient digestion of food.

Anatomy of Breathing

The structure or anatomy of how the breath originates is important to understand in order to gain the most benefit from breathing. Breathing is a unique function of the body in that it can be either voluntary or involuntary. If you think about it, you can control how fast or how deep you breathe. If you ignore your breathing, your body has an involuntary mechanism that allows you to keep breathing, even when you are asleep. It is impossible to do this with your heart or intestines or any other organ system, for that matter. In other words, you can't voluntarily make your heart beat slower or your stomach digest food faster. This is significant because changing the rate or depth of your breathing allows you to tap into the mechanism that improves your circulation as well as your overall sense of well-being. In practicing SignChiDo, we will incorporate this concept of breathing into every posture and movement, which will result in a stronger, healthier body. Let's take a closer look at how air is moved into and out of the incredible machine we call the human body.

The Nose

The nose is a very important structure required for breathing. It is divided into the right and left nasal cavity by the nasal septum. Each nasal cavity contains its own respiratory area and olfactory (or smell) area. The nose has five functions. The first function is to direct air into the respiratory tract. It acts as a gathering site to move air into the body. Secondly, the nose is where we as humans experience the sense of smell (or olfactory). Third, the nose acts as a dust filtrator. The little hairs that grow inside the nose filter the air as we breathe. Fourth, the nose serves to humidify the air. As air passes through the respiratory area in the nose, the air is warmed and moistened before it passes through to the lungs. This helps maintain a constant temperature of the air in order to prevent damage to the sensitive lung tissue. And lastly, the nose receives secretions from the sinuses.

While practicing SignChiDo, it is very important to make sure to inhale though your nose and not your mouth. When you exhale, it is optional to breath out either through your nose or your mouth.

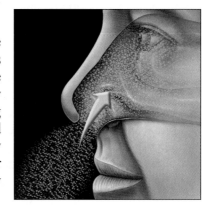

The position of your tongue during diaphragmatic breathing is often overlooked. The tongue should be relaxed, resting gently behind the front teeth, touching the roof of your mouth. The speed at which you breathe is ultimately controlled at the level of your nose. Your breath should be slow and constant.

The shape of the nose plays an important role in preparing the air before it reaches the lungs. A long, big nose is ideal for cooler, dry climates because it allows more time to warm and moisten the air before it reaches the lungs. People who live in the Middle East, for example, benefit from this characteristic. On the other hand, a warm, humid climate, such as in tropical jungles, requires less processing of the air. Therefore, the wide, open nostril nose is characteristic in that climate.

The inside lining of the nose serves the important function of preventing the loss of heat and moisture from the body during exhalation. If you are practicing breathing exercises in a cool or dry climate, I would recommend that you exhale through your nose. This will prevent loss of heat in the cold as well as maintain moisture thus preventing dehydration in a dry climate. On the other hand, if it is very warm and humid, I would recommend that you exhale through your mouth. This will help get rid of excess heat so you don't get overheated during your exercise.

The Respiratory Tract

Once air enters through the nose, the air is moved along the respiratory tract ultimately reaching the lungs. The respiratory tract is made up of the trachea, bronchi, smaller branches of bronchi called bronchioles, and small air sacs called alveoli that branch into the lung. The trachea is a smooth tube-like structure that begins at the level of the throat. The bronchi split into smaller and smaller branches that resemble the appearance of a tree. The

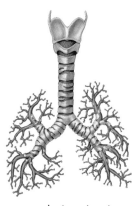

respiratory tract

small branches of this so-called "bronchial tree" eventually lead into small air sac alveoli. At the level of the alveoli, air is exchanged in the lung. The oxygen that we breathe in is exchanged for carbon dioxide, which is expelled when we breathe out. The average person has about three hundred

alveoli in lungs

million alveoli in his or her lungs. During diaphragmatic breathing, it is important to breathe at a slow steady pace allowing enough time for all of those tiny alveoli sacs to expand with oxygen. It is often beneficial to pause after a deep inhalation to visualize those little sacs expanding with air. Finally, when all this oxygen accumulates in the lungs, it is carried by the red blood cells to the rest of the body.

heart and lungs

The Lungs

The human lung is a soft, spongy organ. It is shaped like a cone and is very elastic. The right lung is larger and heavier than the left lung. Each lung is contained within its own sac in the chest cavity with the heart located between them in the middle of the chest. The many millions of alveoli described above cover the inner lining of the lungs. This is where the lungs take up oxygen.

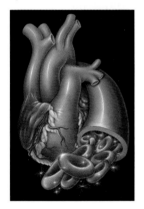

oxygen in vessels

With each breath, oxygen is removed from the air and transported to the blood stream to be pumped out to the rest of the body. The deeper a person breathes, the more the lungs expand resulting in more oxygen. The more oxygen the blood carries, the more relaxed the blood vessels will be. When the blood vessels are relaxed, they expand, or dilate, allowing more blood to flow. This is a very important concept in lowering blood pressure, decreasing risk for heart disease, enhancing memory, and reducing chronic fatigue symptoms.

There are many factors that can affect or limit your lungs' ability to deliver oxygen to the rest of your body. Inhaling fumes, cigarette smoke, or any other type of toxin in the air can affect your lungs' function. Instead of the blood vessels expanding, they constrict, which results in less blood flow, leading to higher blood pressure, increased risk for heart disease due to less blood flowing

blood vessel expanding

to the heart, poor memory due to less blood flowing to the brain, and worse muscle fatigue due to less blood flowing to the muscles.

As a physician, I would highly discourage you from practicing deep-breathing exercises in a smoke-filled environment or a polluted area with a lot of traffic. Think of the air as nourishment to the lung. If you breathe in dirty air, then the lung function will ultimately suffer, resulting in potential illness.

blood vessel constricting

As we prepare to practice diaphragmatic breathing, keep in mind the anatomy of your breath. Visualize the air moving into your nose, down the respiratory tract through the bronchial tree, and into your lungs. Imagine those little alveoli sacs expanding with each breath. Keep in mind the movement of your diaphragm as you breathe. Feel your entire lung expand as you inhale and contract as you exhale. The diaphragm moves down as you inhale, and moves up as you exhale.

When practicing SignChiDo, the movements should be intentionally coordinated with breathing. As your breathing becomes deeper, your movements should become slower. The coordination of your movement with breathing is based on the change in the direction of the movement. For example, when you raise your arms up, you should inhale. When you lower your arms, you should exhale. The next section will outline basic diaphragmatic breathing exercises with movement. This will be our routine SignChiDo warm up.

Breathing Exercises

Watch your breath

Close your eyes, and watch your breath. As you inhale through your nose, feel the cool air entering in. Exhale gently through the nose, and feel the warm air flowing out. Focus on the breath at the nostrils. Repeat for five full breaths.

Once you feel comfortable focusing on the nostrils, begin visualizing the air as it moves all the way down the respiratory tree and into the lungs. "Feel" and "watch" every part of your lung expand as you inhale, especially the lower lungs. Force even the last bit of air into the lungs as you inhale. Hold the breath for three seconds, and then exhale. When you exhale, allow the lungs to naturally deflate without forcing the process. Repeat five full breaths. This exercise can be done at any time and in any place lying, seated, or standing.

Belly breathing (diaphragmatic breathing)

Close your eyes, and relax your mind and body. Assume a comfortable position lying, seated, or standing. Inhale through the nose, and exhale through the mouth. Place your hands on the lower abdomen. As you inhale, imagine the air moving down causing the diaphragm to move downward. This causes the belly to protrude forward or expand like a balloon. As you exhale, the diaphragm moves upward, and the belly moves in or deflates like a balloon. Feel the belly moving in and out as you breathe. Repeat five full breaths.

Diaphragmatic Breathing Relaxercises

Important Points:

- All movements must be slow and deliberate.

- Focus your mind on connecting your breath to the arm movements so that the arms stop at the same time the breath stops.

- Allow each arm movement to flow into the next without pausing.

- Lead each arm movement with the palms of your hand.

- When you complete the last arm movement of "inside palms down," as you exhale with the arms moving downward, let your body sink by bending your knees at the same time. Hold the position for 3 to 5 seconds; repeat 3 times.

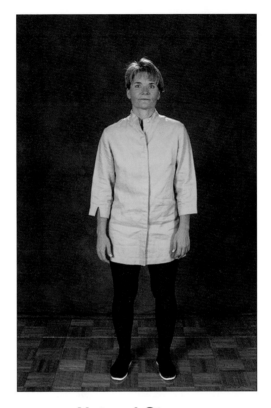

Natural Stance

Footprint: Feet shoulder width apart, flat on the ground, toes facing forward.
Weight distribution: Equal weight distribution with knees slightly bent.

Diaphragmatic Breathing Relaxercises

Arms out in front of the body, "Palms up, palms down"

Breathe in: Start with arms hanging down at the level of the hips. With both palms facing forward raise in unison to above the shoulder height.

Breathe out: Turn both palms downward and lower arms in unison to the level of the hips.

♡Diaphragmatic Breathing Relaxercises

Arms out to the side of the body, "Palms up, palms down"

Breathe in: Turn both palms upward and raise hands in unison to above the shoulder height (arms extended out to the side).

Breathe out: Turn both palms downward and lower hands in unison to the level of the hips.

♡Diaphragmatic Breathing Relaxercises

"Inside palms up, inside palms down"

Breathe in: Start with arms straight down by your side, with hands at the level of your belly button, both palms turned upward. In unison, raise both palms upward to the level of the chest with the elbows extended out to the side.

Breathe out: In unison, turn both palms downward and move hands down. The elbows remain extended out to the side.

♡Diaphragmatic Breathing Relaxercises

Variation-Seated Position

Breathe in:

Breathe out:

Notes

Chapter 3

Posture

Posture

T he stances and postures practiced in SignChiDo are designed to correlate with the body's natural structure. The proper alignment of the body will not only strengthen the muscles, but also prevent injury by avoiding unnecessary strain to the joints and ligaments that support the body.

When practicing SignChiDo, it is important to align the body according to the four curvatures of the spine. The adult spinal column consists of thirty-three vertebrae, of which twenty-four are moveable. These twenty-four vertebrae need to be properly aligned in order to gain the most benefit from SignChiDo. Whether you are practicing lying, seated, or standing, it is important to learn how to align your head, shoulders, hips, knees, and feet so that the muscles surrounding the spine are relaxed.

The first curvature of the spine is the **cervical curve** (neck curve). It consists of seven vertebrae. This is the most flexible area of the spine and therefore plays an important role in posture. Since the head rests on the cervical spine, we will pay close attention to proper positioning of the head. When practicing SignChiDo, imagine the head

adult spinal column

suspended from above. An imaginary line should connect your shoulder with the opening to your ear. Giving thought to this imaginary line will prevent the head from protruding forward, which will decrease muscle tension in the shoulders and upper back. Forward head posture (F.H.P.) is one of the most common postural problems.

20

When the head is straight and upright, three important things occur. First, air is moved into and out of the lungs more easily. Second, blood flow to the brain is smooth and uninterrupted. And third, the body's chi (internal energy) is enhanced.

head posture and
air flow

The second curvature of the spine is the **thoracic curve** (mid-back curve). It consists of twelve vertebrae. Because the thoracic spine supports the rib cage, it has limited movement. To maintain the proper curvature of the thoracic spine, it is important to allow the rib cage to hang down naturally. This will help strengthen the muscles and ligaments attached to the vertebrae. Most people think that proper posture is achieved by expanding the chest upward. This goes against gravity and works in opposition to the normal curvature of the spine. When practicing SignChiDo, allow the shoulders and chest to be relaxed hanging down but not forward. This posture will allow for easier movement of the rib cage resulting in less muscle tightness and deeper breathing.

The third curvature of the spine is the **lumbar curve** (low back curve). It consists of five vertebrae. This is closely related to the fourth curve, called the sacral curvature, which is immobile. I will refer to this low-back area as the lumbo-sacral curvature. It is the lumbo-sacral area, or pelvis, that supports the weight of the body and is the strongest area of the entire spinal column. This is also where the body's center of gravity is located. (The body's center of gravity lies two inches in front of the second sacral vertebrae, or the width of four fingers below the navel).

The alignment of the hips, knees, and feet is important in order to maintain the proper lumbo-sacral curvature. The hips should be in alignment with the shoulders. The feet should be shoulder width apart so that they are in alignment with the hips. The knees should be slightly bent to prevent excess strain to the knee joint. This slight bend of the knee prevents displacement of the center of gravity during transitional movements.

The effects of posture on health are becoming more and more evident. Headache, spinal pain, high blood pressure, poor circulation, and poor lung capacity are among the functions that can be improved by proper posture. When practicing SignChiDo, relax the pelvis and stand firm. The head should be upright in proper alignment with the shoulder to avoid the (F.H.P.) forward head posture. When this proper posture is maintained, all the muscles around the spine will be relaxed, thus decreasing the amount of energy expended to hold the body upright.

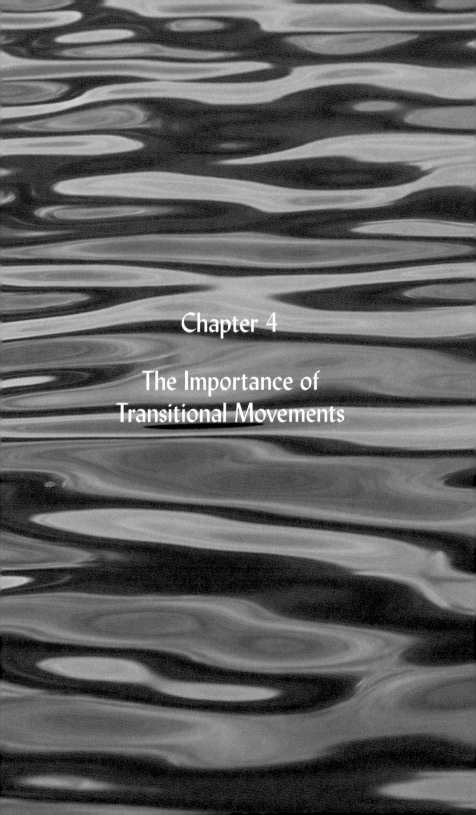

Chapter 4

The Importance of
Transitional Movements

T ransitional movement refers to the movement between postures. During the transitional movement, breathing and proper alignment of the body become essential. Breathing is an integral part of the transitional movement in SignChiDo. Each movement should be performed as if your breath were responsible for initiating that movement. In other words, your movements should be intentionally coordinated with your breathing. The amount of time it takes you to inhale should be the same amount of time it takes you to move from one position to the next. The movement and breath should pause at the same time only to flow into the next movement.

Proper alignment of your body means standing or sitting in an upright, balanced, comfortable position. It is a position that you must become accustomed to in order to strengthen the muscles that support your spine, which ultimately will prevent injury. When the body's posture is poor, the ligaments and tendons that support the spine become strained. Over time, these damaged ligaments and tendons result in pain and spasms, which can lead to osteoarthritis if not corrected.

There are two ways in which SignChiDo helps to prevent injuries. First, it strengthens muscle. The slow, controlled pivoting motions practiced in SignChiDo strengthen the core muscles that support the spine.

When moving from one posture to another, it is important not to bob up and down. This will keep your body's center of gravity (which is located four finger widths below your navel) at a constant level, thus preventing unnecessary strain to the low back area. You can accomplish this by shifting your weight from one leg to the other before stepping and always keeping one knee bent. Bobbing occurs when you straighten the knee prior to stepping into the next stance. When the center of gravity changes, we lose our balance. This leads us to the next important point in preventing injuries, which is proper balance.

Proper balance is very important in preventing injuries. When your body is balanced, it is highly unlikely that you will fall down. Injuries occur when the body falls off balance. SignChiDo was designed to improve balance by introducing the concept of shifting stances. Shifting your weight repetitively from one stance to another stimulates the brain's proprioceptive mechanism. This proprioceptive mechanism is responsible for gathering input from the muscles and joints, then translating that information so that we can sense the position of our body while at rest, as well as with movement. Practicing SignChiDo will improve balance by strengthening this proprioceptive mechanism in the brain so that we become more aware of our own body.

In conclusion, the transitional movements practiced in SignChiDo are what tie everything together. Each posture that depicts a word is tied to the next word through the transitional movement. With repetition and practice, these movements will become automatic. This will allow you to direct all of your attention toward feeling and visualizing the words demonstrated in your movement.

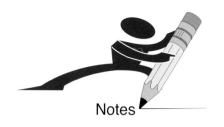

Notes

Chapter 5

What Is Chi?

C hi is the energy that flows when the mind and body are in harmony. In the human body, energy is what creates an electrical impulse that causes the heart to beat. As a result of the heart beating, blood is pumped out to feed the rest of the body including the brain. As this blood flows in the vessels, along with it flows a certain amount of that electrical impulse or energy. It is this energy that we refer to as "chi."

In order to tap into your chi, you must learn how to sensitize your body so that you can recognize it. Chi flows when the body is relaxed and the mind content. For some people, relaxing is misinterpreted as collapsing. This is not accurate. To relax is to actively intend for your body to respond to that request. For example, deep breathing, when coordinated with slow, deliberate arm movements, has been found to elicit a physiologic response in the body resulting in more oxygen and happier blood vessels. This intended action is the first step toward

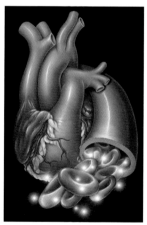

heart - chi flow

sensitizing yourself to the flow of your body's energy source, called "chi." It is important to move slowly so that your mind has enough time to assess your body's position.

When practicing SignChiDo, I encourage you to follow a three-step pattern that will help to harmonize your mind and body. This three-step pattern includes first, practicing the slow, rhythmic gestures coordinated with deep breathing. Then, repeat the gestures or word phrase with the intention of visualizing the meaning of the word. The third time, perform the gesture and allow your entire body to feel the significance of that emotion or word as it is being transformed into movement. This routine, which includes breathing, visualization, and sensation, stimulates different parts of the brain to work together. This mental workout when accompanied by physical movement results in a healthier mind and body. When the mind and body work together, the body's chi becomes stronger, resulting in less muscle fatigue, improved circulation, less depression, a stronger immune system to fight infection, and an overall sense of well-being.

What does chi feel like? It is best described as a warm, heavy sensation often felt in the extremities. Some people may feel a stronger than normal pulse. Remember, chi flows with the blood, therefore, if you increase the flow of chi, in effect you increase blood circulation throughout your body.

As a beginner practicing SignChiDo, you may not experience anything that feels like chi. But with time and repetitious practice, the flow of your chi will strengthen, and you will be able to recognize this source of energy that lives within you. Sign chi do was designed to help you to recognize and channel that energy in a positive, meaningful way.

Chi Exercises

The chi exercises that we will practice in SignChiDo are intended to be organ specific. As a physician, I feel that there is more healing value in directing your attention toward a specific organ, such as the lungs, heart, brain, skin, etc., when practicing these types of exercises.

Chi Exercise for the Lung

Chi Visualization

Focus your mind on the lungs. As you inhale, imagine your chi filling the lungs. Imagine chi as sparkling electricity floating around the blood cells. Feel the warmth of your chi as it reaches your lungs. Feel the healing power of your own chi. Exhale softly, and then repeat this exercise.

Color Visualization

Focus your mind on the lungs. As you inhale, breathe a brilliant white light into your lungs. Visualize this bright light entering into your lungs to illuminate the entire lung. As you exhale, a dark smog-colored light moves out of the lungs leaving behind the bright white light. Feel the nourishment that stays in the lungs along with the white light. As you exhale, visualize any potential disease being carried away from your lungs by the dark-colored light.Repeat this exercise.

Chi Exercises for the Heart

Chi Visualization

Become aware of your heart. As you inhale, imagine your chi filling the heart. Feel the warm chi penetrate the heart muscle from inside the heart. Feel the heart pump more strongly because of this nourishment. Exhale softly through your mouth, leaving all of your chi in the heart to be pumped out to the rest of the body. Repeat this exercise.

Color Visualization

Become aware of your heart. As you inhale, visualize a bright red light filling the heart. As you exhale, imagine a dirty, dark red color leaving your body through your breath. With each breath, the heart fills with a brighter glowing red as the dark polluted color leaves your body. Repeat this exercise.

These chi exercises should be done at the end of your practice session with your eyes closed. It serves as a warm down to allow you to get in touch with the energy that was generated while practicing the SignChiDo postures.

Chapter 6

Basic SignChiDo Stances

1. Natural Stance

Footprint: Feet shoulder width apart, flat on the ground, toes facing forward.

Weight distribution: Equal weight distribution with knees slightly bent.

2. Straddle Stance

Footprint: Both feet face forward, spread wider apart than natural stance.

Weight distribution: Both knees are bent in a straddle position with weight equal.

3. Front Leaning Stance

Footprint: Front foot approximately one stride in front with foot facing forward. The back foot is slightly turned outward. Both feet flat on floor.

Weight distribution: Front knee bent with 60% weight forward. The back leg is straight.

4. Back Leaning Stance

Footprint: Same as front leaning stance except weight is shifted to the back leg with the back leg bent.

Weight distribution: Back knee bent with 60% weight back. The front leg is straight.

5. Side Leaning Stance

Footprint: Both feet face forward, spread wider apart than the natural stance.

Weight distribution: Bend the right knee with 60% of the weight settled toward the right. Shift weight to the left side with the left knee bent, straightening the right leg.

6. **L-Stance** (back knee bent)

Footprint: Front foot approximately one stride in front of the other with the toes pointing up in the air. Only the heel of the front foot touches the floor. Back foot is turned out forming an "L" shape.

Weight distribution: Most of the weight is settled on the back leg with the knees bent. The front leg is straight.

7. **L-Stance** (front knee bent)

Footprint: Same position,except both feet flat on the floor.
Weight distribution: Weight forward on the front leg with the front knee bent. Back leg is straight.

8. **One-Legged Stance**

Footprint: One foot on the floor with the toes facing forward. The other knee is bent up to the chest position or tucked in behind the knee of the support leg.
Weight distribution: All of the weight on one foot.

Chapter 7

Warm-Up: Shifting Stances

T his section is intended to give you a structured warm-up pattern to build upon as you practice SignChiDo. The warm-up pattern is called "shifting stances." The concept of shifting stances was designed to accomplish several things. First, it allows you to practice all of the stances taught in SignChiDo. This will help you to recall what stances to use when you begin to design your own personal fitness phrases. Next, shifting your weight from one stance to another in a repetitious manner will force you to use different muscle groups that you normally would not use. This will strengthen the muscles in the legs, buttocks, hips, and low back area resulting in improved balance. This warm up is not very time consuming and can be done nearly anywhere. For example, you can shift your weight back and forth while waiting in line at the airport, grocery store, or restaurant, or even while getting your oil changed. The more you practice these stances, the sooner they will become automatic. Eventually you will be able to do them without even thinking.

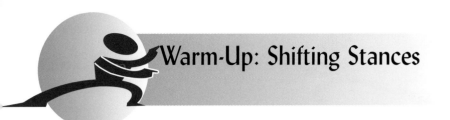
Front Stance - Back Stance - Front Stance

Natural Stance Start

Step forward with the right leg into
Front Leaning Stance

Shift weight back to
Back Leaning Stance

Shift weight forward to
Front Leaning Stance

Step back to Natural Stance.
Repeat the exercise stepping with the opposite leg.

Side Stance - Side Stance - Straddle Stance

Natural Stance Start

Step to the right side with
the right leg into
Side Leaning Stance

Shift weight to the
left side into
Side Leaning Stance

Shift weight to the
center into
Straddle Stance

Step up to Natural Stance.
Repeat the exercise stepping with the opposite leg.

"L" Stance: Back - Forward - Back

Natural Stance Start

Step back with the right leg
into **"L" Stance**, weight back

Shift weight forward to
"L" Stance, weight forward

Shift weight back to
"L" Stance, weight back

Step up to Natural Stance.
Repeat the exercise stepping with the opposite leg.

One-Legged Stance

Natural Stance Start

Shift all of your weight to the left leg. Raise the right knee up to the front (thigh parallel to the floor). Hold for 3 seconds.

Then curl the right foot in behind the left knee. Hold for 3 seconds.

Step down to Natural Stance.
Repeat the exercise stepping with the opposite leg.

SIGN CHI DŌ

The shifting stance relaxercises are unique to Sign Chi Do. They are called relaxercises because they are exercises that help us to "actively" relax. The slow, rhythmic arm movements that were used when practicing deep diaphragmatic breathing are the same movements applied here. We've just taken the technique one step further. That is, by combining the breathing and arm movements with shifting stances.

This type of exercise enhances circulation while at the same time calms the mind. It should be used as part of your warm-up exercise to prepare your mind and body so that you get the most out of your practice. The shifting stance relaxercises should also be done as a cool down exercise. It allows your entire being to come together by harmonizing your breathe with the rhythmic movement of your arms and legs.

Front Stance - Back Stance - Front Stance

Natural Stance Start

Step forward with the right leg into **Front Leaning Stance**

INHALE - Both arms in front, palms facing upward, rise in unison to shoulder level.

Shifting Stance Relaxercises

Front Stance - Back Stance - Front Stance

Turn palms down to face the ground

Shift weight back to **Back Leaning Stance**

EXHALE - Palms turn down, both arms move down in unison to hip level with palms facing the back.

Front Stance - Back Stance - Front Stance (cont.)

Shift weight forward to front leaning stance

INHALE - Both arms in front, palms facing upward, rise in unison to shoulder level.

Front Stance - Back Stance - Front Stance (cont.)

Step back to natural stance

EXHALE - Palms turn down, both arms move down in unison to stop in front of the body at hip level, palms facing the ground.

REPEAT starting with opposite leg.

47

Side Stance - Side Stance - Straddle Stance

Natural Stance Start

Step to the right side with the right leg into
Side Leaning Stance.

INHALE - Both arms extended out to the right side, palms facing upward, rise in unison to shoulder level.

48

Side Stance - Side Stance - Straddle Stance (cont.)

Turn palms down to face the ground.

Shift weight to the left side into **Side Leaning Stance.**

EXHALE - Palms turned down, both arms move down in unison to stop in front of the body at hip level.

49

Side Stance - Side Stance - Straddle Stance (cont.)

Shift weight to center into **Straddle Stance**

INHALE - Start at the level of your belly button, both palms turned upward. In unison, both palms rise upward to the level of the chest with the elbows extended out to the side.

Shifting Stance Relaxercises

Side Stance - Side Stance - Straddle Stance
(cont.)

EXHALE - Palms turned down, both arms move down in unison to stop at hip level.

Side Stance - Side Stance - Straddle Stance (cont.)

Step up to **Natural Stance**

INHALE - Both palms turned upward and rise in unison to shoulder level.

EXHALE - Both palms turned downward and lower in unison to the level of the hips.

REPEAT starting with opposite leg.

"L" Stance: Back - Forward - Back

Natural Stance Start

Step back with the right leg into **L Stance.**

INHALE - Both arms in front, palms facing upward rise in unison to shoulder level.

"L" Stance: Back - Forward - Back
(cont.)

Palms turn down. Shift weight forward to **L Stance**

EXHALE - Palms turn down, both arms move down in unison to stop in front of the body at hip level, palms facing the ground.

"L" Stance: Back - Forward - Back
(cont.)

Shift weight back to **L Stance**

INHALE - Both arms in front, palms facing upward, rise in unison to shoulder level.

"L" Stance: Back - Forward - Back (cont.)

Step up to **Natural Stance**

EXHALE - Palms turn down, both arms move down in unison to hip level with palms facing the floor.

56

Shifting Stance Relaxercises

One Legged Stance

Shift all weight to the left leg.
Raise the right knee up to the front with the thigh parallel
to the floor.

*INHALE - Both arms in front, palms facing upward rise in unison
to shoulder level.*

One Legged Stance (cont.)

Palms turned downward, place the right palm on top of the back of the left hand. Curl the right foot behind the left knee with the left knee bent.

EXHALE - Both hands move down together to the level of the abdomen. Hold for 3 seconds.

Step down to natural stance. Repeat on the other side.

Chapter 8

SignChiDo Word Groups
Intro Set

"Be Open Minded"
"Be Encouraged" or "Motivated"
"Be Sincere" or "Authentic"
"To Concentrate" or "Be Focused"
"To Aim" or "Persevere"
"To Declare" or "Make Up One's Mind"
"To Want" or "Desire"

Word Groups - Intro Set

T he postures that we will practice in SignChiDo are divided into four groups of words. Each posture depicts a different word. When you practice these word postures, it is important to focus all of your attention on how the arm movements actually define the meaning of that word. In this section, Emot, the SignChiDo mascot, will help you remember each posture as it defines the word. For example, Emot will say "Imagine expanding the mind" as you move your arms out to depict the word "open-minded."

Emot

When practicing SignChiDo postures, I suggest that you follow a three-step pattern. First, practice the slow rhythmic gesture of the word coordinated with deep breathing. Then, repeat the gesture with the intention of "visualizing" the meaning of that word or phrase. And finally, perform the gesture, and allow your entire body to "feel" the significance of that word or emotion as it is being transformed into movement. Once you've learned all of the words, you can then start mixing and matching different postures and words with stances to create your own personalized fitness phrase.

You will discover, there is no right or wrong way to do it. You can step in any direction using any stance to design your own exercise phrase. If you wish to add another dimension to your relaxation exercise, say the word or phrase out loud. This is a powerful tool to help you stay focused and improve concentration. SignChiDo was designed for you ultimately to take ownership of and create what works best for you. So let's do it!

Word Groups - Intro Set

"BE OPEN MINDED"

Raise both fisted hands up to the head, just in front of the temples with palms facing inward.
INHALE THROUGH THE NOSE AS YOU MOVE ARMS UP.

Extend the arms up and outward in a "V" shape with palms facing up. Elbows straight but not locked out.
EXHALE THROUGH THE MOUTH AS YOU EXTEND THE ARMS UP AND OUT.

"Imagine expanding the mind"

"BE ENCOURAGED" OR "MOTIVATED"

Pull both elbows back with the palms open facing outward. The hands should rest next to your ribs.
INHALE THROUGH THE NOSE AS YOU PULL THE ARMS IN NEXT TO THE BODY.

Simultaneously, push both hands straight forward with the palms leading the way and thumbs pointed up to the sky.
EXHALE THROUGH THE MOUTH YOU EXTEND THE ARMS FORWARD.

"Imagine encouraging someone along by the gesture of pushing forward gently"

"BE SINCERE" OR "AUTHENTIC"

Raise the index finger of the right hand up to rest on the lips. The closed palm of the right hand faces left.
INHALE THROUGH THE NOSE AS YOU MOVE THE RIGHT INDEX FINGER UP IN A SMALL ARC-LIKE MOTION.

Continue the arc like motion forward with the index finger pointing upward and out.
EXHALE THROUGH THE MOUTH AND EXTEND THE RIGHT INDEX FINGER UP AND OUT IN AN ARC-LIKE MOTION.

"Imagine coming directly from the lips as being the truth"

63

Word Groups - Intro Set

"TO CONCENTRATE" OR "BE FOCUSED"

With both palms open facing in toward each other, raise both hands up to the sides of the face, as if to put blinders on. **INHALE THROUGH THE NOSE AS YOU MOVE BOTH HANDS UP.**

Extend both arms out to the front in unison. **EXHALE THROUGH THE MOUTH AS YOU EXTEND THE ARMS FORWARD.**

"Imagine directing your attention forward"

"TO AIM" OR "PERSEVERE"

Extend the left arm forward to eye level with the index finger pointed out. At the same time raise the right arm to point the index finger toward the head.
INHALE THROUGH THE NOSE AS YOU MOVE BOTH ARMS UP INTO POSITION.

Keeping the left arm still, extend the right arm so the right index finger deliberately touches the left index finger
EXHALE SOFTLY THROUGH THE MOUTH AS YOU MOVE THE RIGHT FINGER FORWARD TO TOUCH THE STATIONARY LEFT FINGER.

"Imagine thought directed outward toward a goal"

65

"TO DECIDE" OR "MAKE UP ONE'S MIND"

Raise both hands up to touch the forehead with the index fingers.
INHALE THROUGH THE NOSE AS YOU MOVE THE ARMS UP.

Extend both hands forward, the elbows slightly bent. (The index finger and thumb touch creating a small circle. The palms are facing in toward each other.) Maintaining the hand positions, move both arms down in unison to the level of the abdomen.

"Imagine that the mind stops wavering and a precise decision is made"

66

"TO WANT" OR "DESIRE"

Raise both arms forward to shoulder level with palms open to face the sky, elbows slightly bent.
INHALE THROUGH THE NOSE AS YOU EXTEND ARMS OUT.

Gently cup the hands and pull both arms in toward the body. The elbows are bent and tucked in close to the body.
EXHALE THROUGH THE MOUTH AS YOU PULL THE ARMS IN TOWARD THE BODY.

"Imaging grasping something for yourself"

Notes

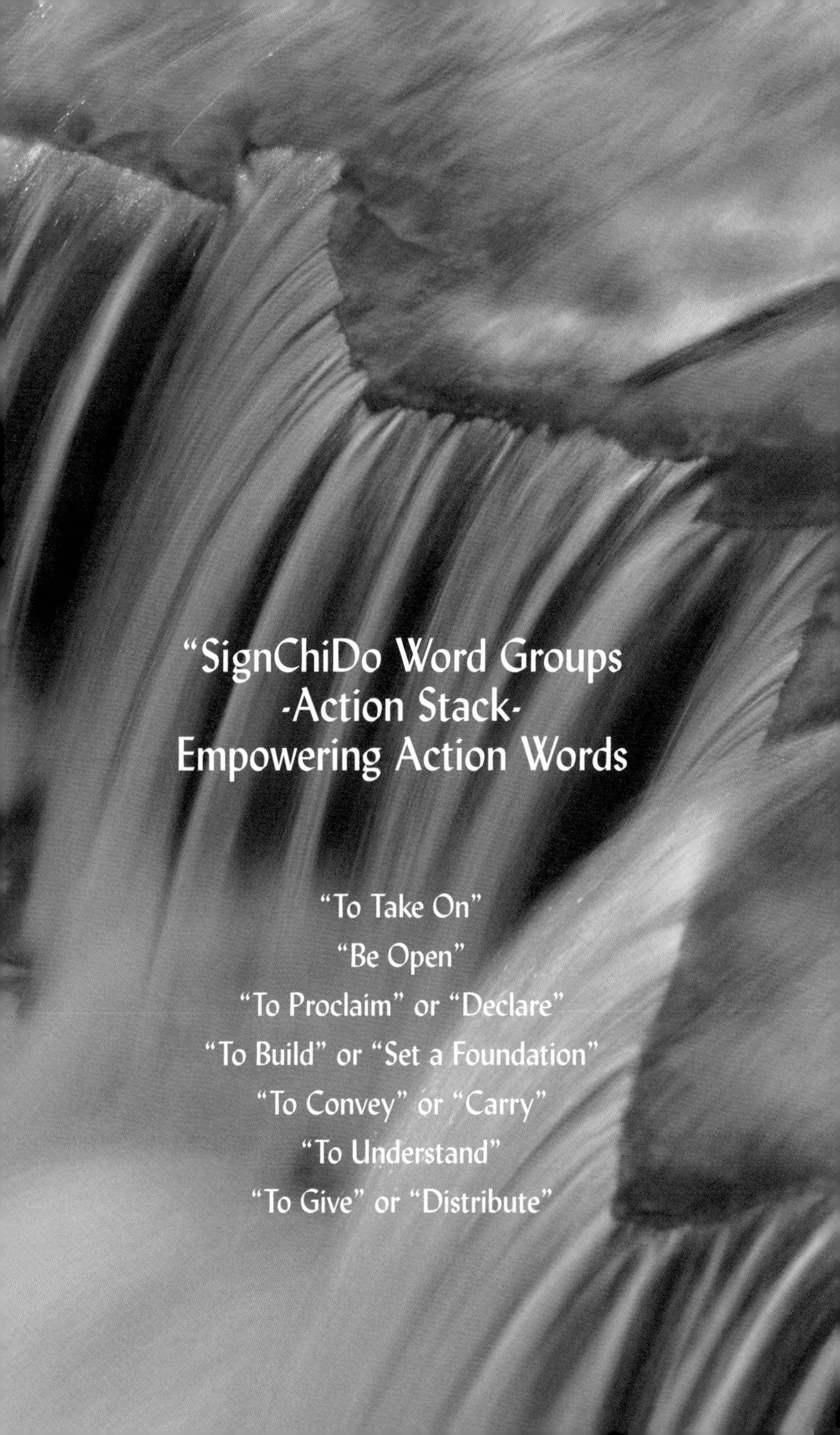

"SignChiDo Word Groups
-Action Stack-
Empowering Action Words

"To Take On"
"Be Open"
"To Proclaim" or "Declare"
"To Build" or "Set a Foundation"
"To Convey" or "Carry"
"To Understand"
"To Give" or "Distribute"

"TO TAKE ON"

Raise both arms forward to shoulder level with palms open facing down.
INHALE THROUGH THE NOSE AS YOU MOVE ARMS UP.

Simultaneously, pull both arms into your chest with a grasping type movement, all four fingers and thumb touching. The elbows are bent in close to your body.
EXHALE THROUGH THE MOUTH AS YOU MOVE ARMS IN TOWARD THE CHEST.

"Imagine taking on or assuming something"

70

"BE OPEN"

Gradually raise arms forward with elbows bent and palms open facing away from you. The index finger edges of each hand are touching.
INHALE THROUGH THE NOSE AS YOU MOVE ARMS UP.

Swing arms apart so the palms are facing in toward you, elbows bent.
EXHALE SOFTLY THROUGH THE MOUTH AS YOU SWING THE ARMS OPEN.

"Imagine being open to something"

71

Action Stack - Empowering Words

"TO PROCLAIM" OR "DECLARE"

Raise both hands to touch the lips with index finger.
INHALE THROUGH THE NOSE AS YOU POINT FINGERS TO THE LIPS.

Rotate hands forward keeping index fingers pointed and extend the arms out.
EXHALE SOFTLY THROUGH THE MOUTH AS YOU EXTEND ARMS OUT.

"Imagine proclaiming something to reach out to many listeners"

72

"TO BUILD" OR "SET A FOUNDATION"

With the right hand positioned below the left hand, raise the arms forward to shoulder level with palms open facing the ground. **INHALE THROUGH THE NOSE AS YOU MOVE ARMS UP.**

Move the right hand in a counterclockwise circular motion under the left palm. The left hand remains still. **EXHALE SOFTLY THROUGH THE MOUTH AS YOU MOVE THE RIGHT HAND IN A CIRCLE.**

"Imagine the area below as the foundation to build upon"

"TO CONVEY" OR "CARRY"

Raise both arms with the palms facing upward to chest level, arms extended forward with elbows slightly bent.
INHALE THROUGH THE NOSE AS YOU MOVE ARMS UP.

Make a small arc motion with the arms in unison to the left side of the body.
EXHALE THROUGH THE MOUTH AS YOU MOVE BOTH ARMS FROM ONE POINT TO ANOTHER.

"Imagine conveying something from one point to another"

74

"TO UNDERSTAND"

Raise the right hand up to the middle of the forehead. The thumb and index fingers are touching facing in toward the forehead.
INHALE THROUGH THE NOSE AS YOU MOVE THE ARM UP TO THE FOREHEAD.

Flick the index finger up and out pointing up.
EXHALE THROUGH THE MOUTH AS YOU FLICK THE INDEX FINGER UP AND OUT.

"Imagine an awakening of the mind depicted by this gesture. It's like a light being 'flicked on' in your mind when you come to understand something"

Action Stack - Empowering Words

"TO GIVE" OR "DISTRIBUTE"

Bring both hands in to rest in front of the heart with the fingertips touching each other.
INHALE THROUGH THE NOSE AS YOU BRING BOTH HANDS IN TO REST IN FRONT OF THE HEART.

Open your arms wide with palms facing up, elbows bent in close to the body.
EXHALE THROUGH THE MOUTH AS YOU OPEN AND EXTEND YOUR ARMS OUT.

"Imagine the gesture of giving"

SignChiDo Word Groups
- Action Stack -
Rejuvenating Action Words

"To Overcome" or "Conquer"
"Tp Protect" or "Defend Against"
"To Give Up" or" Surrender"
"To Apologize"
"To Despise" or "Avoid"
"To Let Go" or "Discard"

"TO OVERCOME" OR "CONQUER"

Raise arms forward to shoulder level. Bend the left arm slightly and extend across the chest with a fist formed. Cock the right fist back. Both wrists are touching.

INHALE THROUGH THE NOSE AS YOU MOVE ARMS INTO POSITION WITH BOTH WRISTS TOUCHING.

Extend the right wrist over and on top of the left wrist. The left arm stays still.

EXHALE SOFTLY THROUGH THE MOUTH AS YOU BEND THE RIGHT WRIST OVER THE LEFT WRIST.

*"Imagine the right hand dominating
the left as if to overcome"*

"TO PROTECT" OR "DEFEND AGAINST"

Bend the elbows of both arms so the fists rest in front of your body at chest level. The arms should be parallel, with the left fist in front of the right.
INHALE THROUGH THE NOSE AS ARMS MOVE INTO POSITION IN FRONT OF THE CHEST.

Both arms move forward a short distance without changing position.
EXHALE THROUGH THE MOUTH AS YOU MOVE ARMS FORWARD.

"Imagine holding firmly as if to protect against something"

"TO GIVE UP" OR "SURRENDER"

Bring both hands in front of the shoulders with palms facing up, with the elbows bent.
INHALE THROUGH THE NOSE AS YOU MOVE HANDS TO THE SHOULDERS.

Push both palms upward toward the sky. Keep elbows slightly bent.
EXHALE SOFTLY THROUGH THE MOUTH AS YOU PUSH BOTH ARMS UPWARD.

"Imagine pushing the hands up in a gesture of giving up or renouncing something"

"TO APOLOGIZE"

Raise the left arm forward to shoulder level with the palm facing up. Simultaneously, place the right fist over the heart and make a circle, with the palm facing inward against your chest.
INHALE THROUGH THE NOSE AS YOU EXTEND THE LEFT ARM FORWARD. MAKE A CIRCLE AGAINST THE CHEST WITH YOUR RIGHT FIST.

Open the right hand and glide it across the palm of the left hand. As the you extend the right hand forward pull the left hand back slightly.
EXHALE THROUGH THE MOUTH AS YOU GLIDE THE RIGHT PALM ACROSS THE LEFT PALM.

"Imagine the gesture of encircling the heart then wiping off a clean slate"

"TO DESPISE" OR "AVOID"

Raise both hands up to rest at shoulder level with elbows bent and palms facing away from the body.
INHALE THROUGH THE NOSE AS YOU PULL BOTH HANDS IN FRONT OF THE SHOULDERS WITH PALMS FACING OUTWARD.

Push both hands forward with the palms facing away from the body. The elbows stay slightly bent.
EXHALE THROUGH THE MOUTH AS YOU PUSH BOTH PALMS FORWARD.

"Imagine the gesture to push away or avoid something"

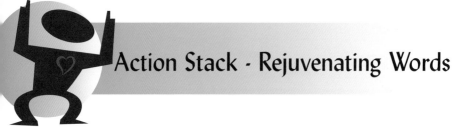

"TO LET GO" OR "DISCARD"

Raise both fists up to chest level with palms facing inward.
INHALE THROUGH THE NOSE AS YOU PULL YOUR ARMS UP TO THE CHEST.

Swing both arms slightly downward then up and out with both palms facing the sky. Direct the arms toward the right with the right arm higher than the left arm.
EXHALE THROUGH THE MOUTH AS YOU SWING THE ARMS OUTWARD.

"Imagine the gesture of tossing something up and out"

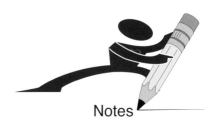

Notes

SignChiDo Word Groups
- Emotions in Motion -
Warm Emotions

"Love"

"Peace" or "Calmness"

"Good Health" or "Strength"

"Contentment"

"Freedom" or "Independence"

"Humility" or "Humbleness"

"Honesty"

"LOVE"

Raise both arms forward with the palms open facing up.
INHALE THROUGH THE NOSE AS YOU MOVE ARMS UP.

Pull both hands in to be placed over the heart with the right palm resting on top of the left hand.
EXHALE THROUGH THE MOUTH AS YOU PULL BOTH HANDS IN TO REST ON THE HEART.

"Imagine embracing the heart"

"PEACE" OR "CALMNESS"

Raise both hands to rest in front of the mouth with palms open facing inward.
INHALE THROUGH THE NOSE AS YOU MOVE THE HANDS INTO POSITION.

Simultaneously, move both arms downward and out with the palms facing the ground. The elbows remain slightly bent as arms extend down and out.
EXHALE THROUGH THE MOUTH AS YOU MOVE THE ARMS DOWN AND OUT ON AN ANGLE WITH PALMS FACING THE GROUND.

"Imagine the gesture for quiet and calmness"

"GOOD HEALTH" OR "STRENGTH"

Place both palms against the chest.
INHALE THROUGH THE NOSE AS YOU PLACE BOTH HANDS ON YOUR CHEST.

Form hands into fists as you move your arms away from the body forcefully. The right arm extended with the elbow slightly bent and the left arm held in closer to the body (assume the boxer's pose).
EXHALE THROUGH THE MOUTH AS YOU MOVE THE ARMS OUTWARD.

"Imagine strength emanating from the body"

"CONTENTMENT"

Raise both hands to rest against the chest with the elbows bent and palms facing the ground. The right hand is above the left hand.
INHALE THROUGH THE NOSE AS YOU MOVE BOTH HANDS INTO POSITION IN FRONT OF THE CHEST WITH PALMS FACING DOWN.

Slowly slide both hands down along the front of the body to stop at waist level. Keep the hands in position with the right hand above the left.
EXHALE THROUGH THE MOUTH AS YOU PUSH BOTH HANDS DOWNWARD.

"Imagine the inner feelings settling down"

"FREEDOM" OR "INDEPENDENCE"

Raise both arms up to the chest with the arms crossed and fists facing inward.

INHALE THROUGH THE NOSE AS YOU PULL BOTH ARMS INTO THE CHEST WITH FISTS FACING INWARD.

Swing open the arms with the fists facing outward. Arms extended with the elbows slightly bent.

EXHALE THROUGH THE MOUTH AS YOU EXTEND THE ARMS OUTWARD ON AN ANGLE IN FRONT OF THE BODY.

"Imagine the gesture of breaking the bonds and being set free"

90

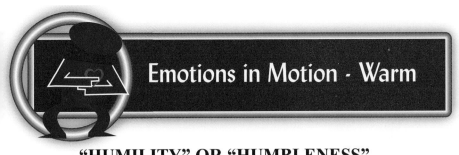

"HUMILITY" OR "HUMBLENESS"

Raise the left arm forward to shoulder level with the palm open facing up. Simultaneously, place the right hand in front of your lips with the palm open and fingers pointed up.
INHALE THROUGH THE NOSE AS YOU MOVE BOTH ARMS INTO POSITION - THE LEFT ARM EXTENDED FORWARD AND RIGHT HAND IN FRONT OF THE MOUTH.

Lower the right hand, keeping fingers pointed up. Circle the left arm in and turn the palm to face down on top of the right fingertips. Press downward with the left palm on top of the right fingers. Nod or bow the head at the same time.
EXHALE THROUGH THE MOUTH AS YOU SETTLE INTO POSITION WITH THE HEAD BOWED AND LEFT HAND PRESSING DOWNWARD ON THE RIGHT HAND.

"Imagine an act of humility or bowing the head"

91

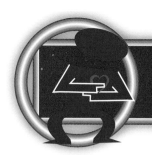

"HONESTY"

Simultaneously, extend the left arm forward to shoulder level with the palm facing up and place the right hand with the index and middle fingers pointing forward in front of the right shoulder. **INHALE THROUGH THE NOSE AS YOU MOVE THE ARMS INTO POSITION.**

Glide the right index and middle finger along the palm of the left hand. As the right arm extends away from your body, pull the left arm in toward your body. **EXHALE THROUGH THE MOUTH AS YOU EXTEND THE RIGHT HAND OVER THE LEFT PALM IN A STRAIGHT LINE**

*"Imagine following a straight and true path
as depicted by the gesture"*

SignChiDo Word Groups
- Emotions in Motion -
Cool Emotions

'Depression"

"Procrastination"

"Doubt" or "Disbelief"

"Greed" or "Selfishness"

"Fight" or "Terrorism"

"DEPRESSION"

Place both open hands on the chest with the fingers facing downward.
INHALE THROUGH THE NOSE AS YOU MOVE THE HANDS INTO POSITION.

Slide both hands down the body to stop at waist level.
EXHALE THROUGH THE MOUTH AS YOU SLIDE YOUR HANDS DOWN AGAINST YOUR BODY.

"Imagine the inner feelings 'down' or 'depressed'

94

"PROCRASTINATION"

Raise the hands to chest level with the elbows bent. The index fingers and thumbs are touching and the hands are open with the rest of the fingers pointing forward.
INHALE THROUGH THE NOSE AS YOU RAISE THE HANDS TO CHEST LEVEL.

Simultaneously, move both hands forward in a series of two short stepping motions.
EXHALE THROUGH THE MOUTH AS YOU EXTEND THE ARMS FORWARD IN SMALL CIRCULAR-TYPE MOTIONS.

"Imagine putting things off by moving them into the future repeatedly"

"DOUBT" OR "DISBELIEF"

Raise the right arm forward to shoulder level with a fisted palm facing the ground (the left arm remains extended down). **INHALE THROUGH THE NOSE AS YOU MOVE THE RIGHT ARM UP.**

Simultaneously, raise the left arm forward to shoulder level as you move the right arm downward. **EXHALE THROUGH THE MOUTH AS YOU MOVE THE LEFT ARM UP AND THE RIGHT ARM DOWN.**

"Imagine wavering the arms as if in doubt or disbelief"

"GREED" OR "SELFISHNESS"

Raise both arms forward to shoulder level with palms open facing the ground.
INHALE THROUGH THE NOSE AS YOU MOVE THE ARMS UP.

Slightly bend all ten fingers and in a raking motion pull the arms in toward the chest.
EXHALE THROUGH THE MOUTH AS YOU PULL BOTH ARMS IN TOWARD THE CHEST.

"Imagine grabbing everything for yourself"

"FIGHTING" OR "TERRORISM"

Raise both arms out to the side to shoulder level with fists formed and palms facing up.
INHALE THROUGH THE NOSE AS YOU MOVE ARMS UP.

Move both arms in a circular motion in front of your body and turn the fists palm down to rest in front of your chest, elbows extended out to the side.
EXHALE THROUGH THE NOSE AS YOU CIRCLE THE ARMS IN TO REST IN FRONT OF THE CHEST.

"Imagine the fists in combat"

SignChiDo Word Groups
Closers

"Forever"

"With Confidence"

"The End" or "Finished"

"FOREVER"

With the right index finger pointing forward, make a large clockwise circle in front of the body.
INHALE THROUGH THE NOSE AS YOU TRACE A LARGE CIRCLE.

Bring both hands in toward the chest in front of the shoulders. With the thumb and little fingers pointed out, extend both hands forward in a downward swooping motion to end with the arms extended forward, thumb and little fingers pointed out.
EXHALE THROUGH THE MOUTH AS YOU EXTEND BOTH ARMS FORWARD IN A SWOOPING MOTION.

"Imagine the gesture for around the clock and ahead into the future"

"WITH CONFIDENCE"

Raise both hands up to point to the forehead with the index fingers.
INHALE THROUGH THE NOSE AS YOU MOVE BOTH ARMS UP.

Extend both arms to the front with the hands reaching up as if to grab something. The right hand is above the left. In unison, move both hands down as if to plant an imaginary pole into the ground.
EXHALE THROUGH THE MOUTH AS YOU MOVE BOTH HANDS DOWNWARD AS IF TO PLANT A FLAGPOLE IN THE GROUND.

"Imagine planting one's trust in the gesture of planting a flagpole"

Emotions in Motion · Cool

"THE END" OR "FINISHED"

Raise both palms up to face in toward your head.
**INHALE THROUGH THE NOSE AS YOU MOVE BOTH
HANDS UPWARD.**

In unison, swing both arms out, with the palms turned outward.
**EXHALE THROUGH THE MOUTH AS YOU SWING THE
PALMS TO FACE OUTWARD.**

*"Imagine ridding your hands of something,
indicating the end"*

102

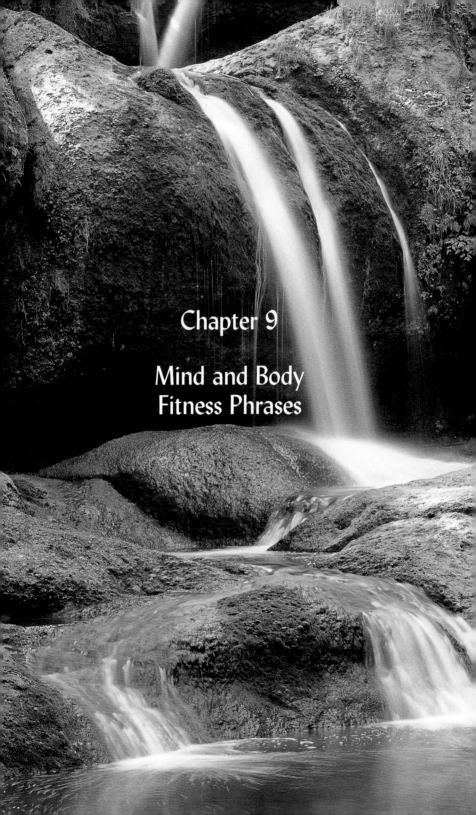

Chapter 9

Mind and Body
Fitness Phrases

T he Mind and Body Fitness Phrases are defined as a group of SignChiDo postures performed in a certain sequence. The four basic principles of SignChiDo, including breathing, posture, transitional movement, and chi flow, come together when practicing the fitness phrases. Deep diaphragmatic breathing ties together the word postures during the transitional period. When slow, rhythmic movements are performed with visualization and feeling, the mind and body unite resulting in chi flow. The more you practice SignChiDo, the clearer this mind and body relationship will be. For example, when you start to notice tension in the body, you will have a way of releasing that tension by making a conscious effort, or intending, to do so.

"Intent" is a word that is very important when practicing SignChiDo, especially when practicing the mind and body fitness phrases. Moving your arms and legs in mid air without intention becomes nothing more than just empty moves. But when you embrace an emotion, then transform that emotion with your entire being into action, unbelievable things start to happen. You begin to feel calm, content, and more focused. Blood pressure improves, circulation improves, your self-image improves, memory becomes sharper, and overall you become more present to yourself and those around you. This occurs because the brain releases chemicals called neuropeptides that are tied to certain emotions. When practicing the fitness phrases, it should be evident how important it is to focus on the intent of the word or emotion that is being performed. With repetition, your ability to focus increases.

The mind and body fitness phrases were designed for you to practice in a repetitious manner. The movements should flow so that you can face different directions without interrupting the pace of your movement or breathing. As you begin to design your own personal fitness phrases, you will experience your emotions transforming into movement. This transformation causes those neuropeptides to be released into the bloodstream. I will talk more about this in the advanced SignChiDo book, but for now, it is important to know that this reaction does occur and the body relies on those chemicals after a while. That is why it is important to know how to practice in 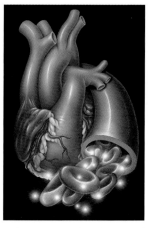 a rhythmic, repetitious manner so you don't interrupt the flow of those chemicals resulting in your body's desire to be in a calm, relaxed state.

I have listed seven different fitness phrases. There is one for each day of the week, however, I would encourage you to begin designing your own creative, empowering expressions that you can put to movement. Remember, take ownership of SignChiDo movements. There is no right or wrong way to do it. So let's just do it!

1. Aim to be humble.

2. Be open minded to let go of procrastination.

3. Desire freedom, despise terrorism.

4. Be sincere to take on love, peace, and contentment.

5. Be motivated to proclaim freedom with confidence.

6. Concentrate on good health; give up depression.

7. Make up your mind to convey love and peace to all.

Aim to be humble

Aim

Begin from the natural stance.
Extend the left arm forward to eye level with the index finger pointed out. At the same time raise the right arm to point the index finger toward the head.
INHALE.

Aim

Step forward with the right leg into front leaning stance. Keeping the left arm still, extend the right arm so the right index finger deliberately touches the left index finger. **EXHALE.**

Aim to be humble

To be humble

Extend the left arm forward to shoulder level with the palm open facing up. Simultaneously, place the right hand in front of your lips with the palm open and fingers pointed upward. **INHALE**.

To be humble

Shift your weight back to the right leg into an "L" stance. Circle the left arm in and turn the palm to face down on top of the right fingertips. Press downward with the left palm on top of the right fingers. Nod your head at the same time you settle your weight back. **EXHALE**.

108

Step up with the right leg into a natural stance. Turn both palms upward and raise in unison to shoulder level. **INHALE**.

Turn both palms downward and lower in unison to the level of the hips. **EXHALE**.

Be open minded

Begin from the natural stance.
Raise both hands up to the head, just in front of the temples with the palms facing inward making a fist. **INHALE**.

Be open minded

Step forward with left leg into front leaning stance. Extend the arms up and outward in a "V" shape with the palms facing upward, elbows straight but not locked out. **EXHALE**.

110

To let go

Step forward with the right leg into front leaning stance. Raise both fists up to chest level with palms facing inward. **INHALE**.

To let go

Swing both arms slightly downward then up and out with both palms facing the sky. Direct the arms toward the right with the right arm higher than the left arm. **EXHALE**.

111

Procrastination

Step forward with the left leg into front leaning stance. Raise the hands to chest level with the elbows bent. The index fingers and thumbs are touching and the hands are open with the rest of the fingers pointing forward. **INHALE**.

Procrastination

Simultaneously, move both hands forward in a series of two short stepping motions. **EXHALE**.

112

Step up with the right leg into a natural stance. Turn both palms upward and raise in unison to shoulder level. **INHALE**.

Turn both palms downward and lower in unison to the level of the hips. **EXHALE**.

Desire freedom, despise terrorism

Desire

Begin from the natural stance.
Raise both arms forward to shoulder level with palms open facing upward. **INHALE**.

Desire

Step back with the left leg into "L" stance. Gently cup the hands and pull both arms in toward the body. The elbows are bent and tucked in close to the body. **EXHALE**.

114

Desire freedom, despise terrorism

Freedom

Shift your weight forward into front leaning stance with the right leg forward. Raise both arms up to the chest with the arms crossed and fists facing inward. **INHALE**.

Freedom

Step up with the left leg into straddle stance. Swing open the arms with the fists facing outward, arms extended with the elbows slightly bent. **EXHALE**.

115

Desire freedom, despise terrorism

Despise

Raise both hands up to rest at shoulder level with elbows bent and palms facing away from the body. **INHALE**.

Despise

Step forward with the right leg into front leaning stance. Push both hands forward with the palms facing away from the body. The elbows are slightly bent. **EXHALE**.

Desire freedom, despise terrorism

Terrorism

Step up with the left leg into straddle stance. Raise arms out to the side to shoulder level with fists formed and palms facing upward. **INHALE**.

Terrorism

Move both arms in a circular motion in front of your body and turn the fists palm down to rest in front of your chest, elbows extended out to the side. Sink into the straddle stance. **EXHALE**.

117

Desire freedom, despise terrorism

Step up with the right leg into a natural stance. Turn both palms upward and raise in unison to shoulder level. **INHALE**.

Turn both palms downward and lower in unison to the level of the hips. **EXHALE**.

Be sincere

Begin from the natural stance.
Raise the index finger of the right hand up to rest on the lips.
The closed palm of the right hand faces the left. **INHALE**.

Be sincere

Step forward with the right leg into front leaning stance.
Continue the arc-like motion forward with the index
finger pointing upward and out. **EXHALE**.

To take on

Extend both arms forward to shoulder level with the palms open facing the ground. **INHALE**.

To take on

Shift your weight back to the left leg into "L" stance. Pull both arms into your chest with a grasping type movement, all four fingers and thumb touching and elbows bent in close to your body. **EXHALE**.

120

Love

Step forward with the left leg into front leaning stance. Raise both arms forward with the palms open facing up. **INHALE.**

Love

Shift your weight back to the right leg into an "L" stance. Pull both hands in and place over the heart with the right palm resting on top of the left hand. **EXHALE.**

Peace

Step back with the left leg into an "L" stance. Raise both hands to rest in front of the mouth with palms open facing inward. **INHALE**.

Peace

Move both arms downward and out with the palms facing the ground. The elbows remain slightly bent. **EXHALE**.

Contentment

Step back with the right leg into the natural position. Raise both hands to rest against the chest with the elbows bent and palms facing the ground. The right hand is above the left hand. **INHALE**.

Contentment

Slowly slide both hands down along the body to stop at waist level. Keep the hands in position, with the right hand above the left. Sink into the natural stance. **EXHALE**.

From a natural stance, turn both palms up and raise in unison to shoulder level. **INHALE**.

Turn both palms downward and lower in unison to the level of the hips. **EXHALE**.

Be motivated

Begin from the natural stance.
Pull both elbows back with the palms open and fingers facing outward. The hands are resting next to your ribs. **INHALE**.

Be motivated

Step forward with the left leg into a front leaning stance. Push both hands forward with the palms leading. The thumbs are pointed upward. **EXHALE**.

125

Proclaim

Step forward with the right leg into front leaning stance. Raise both hands to touch the lips with the index fingers. **INHALE**.

Proclaim

Rotate the hands forward keeping the index fingers pointed and extend the arms to point out. **EXHALE**.

Freedom

Step forward with the left leg into front leaning stance. Raise both arms up to the chest with the arms crossed and fists facing inward. **INHALE**.

Freedom

Swing open the arms with the fists facing outward, arms extended with the elbows slightly bent. **EXHALE**.

127

With confidence

Step up with the right leg into straddle stance. Raise both hands up to point to the forehead with the index fingers. **INHALE**.

With confidence

Extend both arms to the front with the hands reaching up as if to grab something. The right hand is above the left. In unison, move both hands down as if to plant an imaginary pole into the ground. Sink into the straddle stance.
EXHALE as you move arms downward.

128

Step up with the right leg into a natural stance. Turn both palms upward and raise in unison to shoulder level. **INHALE**.

Turn both palms downward and lower in unison to the level of the hips. **EXHALE**.

Concentrate

Begin from the natural stance.
Raise both hands up to the sides of the face with palms open facing in toward each other. **INHALE**.

Concentrate

Step forward with the right leg into front leaning stance. Extend both arms out to the front in unison, elbows slightly bent. **EXHALE**.

130

Good health

Place both palms against the chest. **INHALE.**

Good health

Step forward with the left leg into a front leaning stance. Form both hands into fists as the arms move away from the body forcefully, the right arm extended with the elbow slightly bent and the left arm held in closer to the body. **EXHALE.**

131

Give up

Shift weight back to the right leg into an "L" stance. Bring both hands in front of the shoulders with the palms facing up and the elbows bent. **INHALE**.

Give up

Step back with the left leg into an "L" stance. Push both palms upward. Keep the elbows slightly bent. **EXHALE**.

132

Depression

Step back with the right leg into a natural stance. Place both open hands on the chest with the fingers facing downward. Elbows are bent and extended out to the side. **INHALE.**

Depression

Slide both hands down the body to stop at the waist level, fingers pointing downward, elbows slightly bent. Sink into the natural stance. **EXHALE.**

133

Turn both palms upward and raise in unison to shoulder level. **INHALE**.

Turn both palms downward and lower in unison to the level of the hips. **EXHALE**.

Make up your mind

Begin from the natural stance. Raise both hands up to touch the temples with the index fingers. **INHALE**.

Make up your mind

Extend both hands forward with the elbows slightly bent. The index finger and thumb touch creating a small circle with the palms facing in toward each other. Maintaining the hand positions, move both arms down in unison to the level of the abdomen. Sink in the natural stance. **EXHALE**.

135

Make up your mind to convey love and peace to all

To convey

Raise both arms with the palms facing upward to chest level, arms extended forward with the elbows slightly bent. **INHALE**.

To convey

Step to the side with the right leg into a side leaning stance. Make a small arc motion with the arms in unison to the right side of the body as if to carry something from one point to another. Elbows remain slightly bent.**EXHALE**.

136

Love

Step back with the left leg into an "L" stance. Raise both arms forward with the palms open facing up. **INHALE**.

Love

Pull both hands in and place over the heart with the right palm resting on top of the left hand. **EXHALE**.

Peace

Step back with the right leg into an "L" stance. Raise both hands to rest in front of the mouth with the palms open facing inward. **INHALE**.

Peace

In unison, move both arms downward and out with the palms facing the ground. The elbows remain slightly bent. **EXHALE**.

To all

Step up with the right leg into a natural stance. Both arms circle in front of the body to reach above the head with the palms facing inward. **INHALE**.

To all

Circle both arms out and down as if to embrace the whole world. Palms naturally face upward. **EXHALE**.

Turn both palms upward and raise in unison to shoulder level. **INHALE**.

Turn both palms downward and lower in unison to the level of the hips. **EXHALE**.

Chapter 10

SignChiDo From
A Medical Perspective

"Doc Talk"

"How did "SignChiDo" get its name?"

"How does SignChiDo increase concentration,
heighten spiritual awareness, improve memory,
and enhance an overall sense of well-being?"

"What makes SignChiDo different from other forms
of relaxation and stress reduction exercises?"

"Am I too old to practice SignChi Do?"

"How does SignChiDo decrease blood pressure,
lower heart rate, enhance digestion, and improve
overall circulation?"

"Should pregnant women practice SignChiDo?"

SignChiDo
From A Medical Perspective

How did "SignChiDo" get its name?

The word **"Sign"** represents the universal language of sign that is used throughout this exercise form.

"Chi" is a word that defines the body's inner energy. Documented in medical literature, it flows when the mind and body are in harmony.

"Do." means "the way." It also stands for Doctor of Osteopathic medicine, which is what I am. The essence of this exercise, relaxation form is derived from a medical perspective.

"How does SignChiDo increase concentration, heighten spiritual awareness, improve memory, and enhance an overall sense of well-being?"

The average human brain weighs about four pounds and is approximately the size of a large head of cauliflower. In order to understand the relationship between the brain and SignChiDo, it is important to have an understanding of basic brain functions.

The cerebral cortex, which performs most of the brain's higher

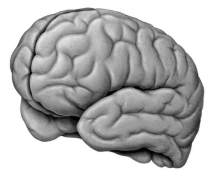

The Human Brain

142

functions, is what distinguishes us human beings from other animals. The cerebral cortex is divided into the left and right hemispheres. Each hemisphere is further divided into four lobes.

- The Frontal lobe is located directly behind the forehead.
- The Temporal lobe is located along the sides of the head.
- The Occipital lobe is located at the back of the head.
- The Parietal lobe sits below the crown of the skull.

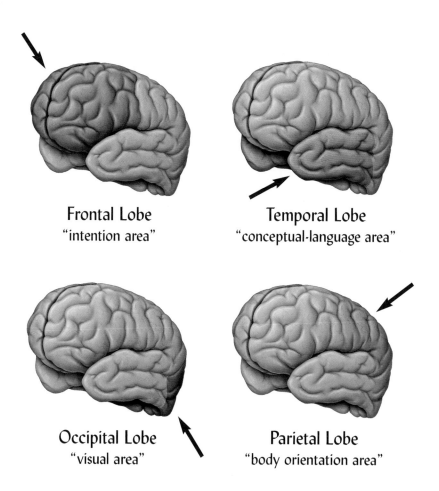

Frontal Lobe
"intention area"

Temporal Lobe
"conceptual-language area"

Occipital Lobe
"visual area"

Parietal Lobe
"body orientation area"

The practice of SignChiDo stimulates each of the four lobes of the brain. The concept of expressing through movement your personal statement or intention by using the universal language of sign stimulates the frontal lobe, temporal lobe, occipital lobe, and parietal lobe. Mental exercise has been found to be very important for the brain. Scientists are realizing that mental exercises, like SignChiDo, cause physical changes in the brain, strengthening the connections between brain cells. This can potentially protect against dementia, according to scientists from Columbia University.

The **frontal lobe** is responsible for the intention of the movement as well as the initiation of muscle activity. The **temporal lobe** is associated with language, in this case the universal language of sign. When practicing SignChiDo, you are encouraged to do visualization and sensory exercises. It is recommended that each word be practiced three times: first, to identify the breathing pattern; second, to visualize the emotion; and third, to actually feel the emotion as you put it into action. This stimulates the **occipital lobe** for visualization and the **parietal lobe** for sensory.

In SignChiDo, the mind and body come together by integrating physical movements with the cognitive thought process of expressing an emotion. This constant connection between all four lobes of the brain allows us to create our self-image and an overall sense of well-being.

Based on medical literature, we believe that these four areas in the brain play an important role in enhancing the mind's ability to concentrate, achieve a heightened spiritual awareness, improve memory, and enhance the overall sense of well-being.

The **frontal lobe**, called the "intention" area, integrates the body movements associated with attaining a goal. It also processes and controls emotions. The intention area of the brain allows us to focus our minds on an idea or emotion. This enhances our ability to concentrate.

The **temporal lobe**, called the "conceptual-language" area, is responsible for abstract concepts as they relate to words. In SignChiDo, we use the abstract universal language of sign movements to depict certain words. For example, the word "open-minded" is depicted by the arms moving up and outward from the head indicating the mind opening outward. This conceptual-language area plays a very important role in spiritual experience and potentially heightens overall spiritual awareness.

The **occipital lobe**, called the visual area, is tied closely to the brain's memory bank. When practicing SignChiDo, the stimulation of this area by visualization and imagery will enhance memory. This type of sensory input is essential for the brain cells to continue to work, reminding us of the saying, "if you don't use it, you lose it." Learning new skills will ultimately increase brain function and improve memory.

The **parietal lobe**, called the body-orientation area, allows us to perceive ourselves in the space with which we exist. In SignChiDo, the changing body orientations or transitional movements stimulate this part of the brain unifying the mind and body. As a result, participants experience an overall sense of well-being.

What makes SignChiDo different from other forms of relaxation and stress reduction exercises?

Instead of emptying your mind, in SignChiDo you are encouraged to fill it with creative, empowering words or emotions that are then communicated through movement. This active process begins in the frontal lobe of the brain (called the intention area). The frontal lobe facilitates nerve fiber activity to enhance your ability to focus more intensely on that emotion or word. This increased nerve fiber activity causes the parietal lobe (body-orientation area) and the occipital lobe (visual area) to fix that word or emotion firmly in your mind so that it becomes real.

With the rhythmic, repetitious practice of SignChiDo, both the mind and body get a workout. Not only are the muscles of your body, including the diaphragm, strengthened, but also thinking about the words and phrases that are transformed into movement constantly stimulates the mind. This mind-body workout is believed to help ward off certain disease processes such as depression, chronic fatigue syndrome, and circulation problems associated with heart disease and diabetes.

The process of learning a new skill such as SignChiDo with the constant thought process involved strengthens the connection between brain cells. Certain brain cells release chemicals that result in a calming effect on the body. The blood pressure is decreased, heart rate slows, and digestion improves. As a result, overall levels of "stress" chemicals decrease.

The physical activity involved in choreographing your own personal statement and transforming it into movement using the universal language of sign improves blood flow to the muscles as well as the brain.

The continuous, rhythmic diaphragmatic breathing practiced in SignChiDo enhances the lung function. This ensures that the blood is rich with oxygen as it nourishes the brain and body. Ultimately, the blood vessels relax and carry oxygen effortlessly to the heart as well as the rest of the body.

Am I too old to practice SignChiDo?

SignChiDo was designed for people of all ages. As we age, the brain, for the most part, remains intact, but some deterioration occurs. The area in the brain that acts as a relay station to pass messages from the memory bank to other parts of the brain-- to move muscles, for example, begins to slow down or become lazy. As a result, muscle coordination declines, perhaps explaining why many older people tend to slow down. This is where SignChiDo can help. This self-paced exercise helps to preserve balance and coordination, if practiced on a daily basis. The repetitive, rhythmic movements serve to strengthen the body from the inside out. No strain is placed on the joints, and SignChiDo can be done standing, sitting, or even lying down. It is a great well-rounded exercise for people of all ages.

How does SignChiDo decrease blood pressure, lower heart rate, enhance digestion, and improve overall circulation?

The practice of SignChiDo stimulates the autonomic nervous system to release certain chemicals that affect the body. The autonomic nervous system is composed of two branches, the parasympathetic system and the sympathetic system. The calm repetitive movements of SignChiDo stimulate the parasympathetic system. As a result, chemicals called neuropeptides are released into the body to conserve energy. This lowers blood pressure and heart rate, promotes digestion, and induces relaxation in the body, especially within the blood vessels to allow for better circulation.

When the blood pressure is controlled, the heart is happier. It is able to pump blood out of the heart to the rest of the body more efficiently. When blood flows more efficiently, the internal organs of the body function better.

Diaphragmatic breathing, which is practiced in SignChiDo, promotes digestion by causing a massaging effect on the intestines with each deep breath. This helps reduce the symptoms of irritable bowel.

Overall, the slow, rhythmic SignChiDo movements, accompanied by deep breathing, stimulate the parasympathetic system to decrease blood pressure, lower heart rate, enhance digestion, and improve overall circulation.

Should pregnant women practice SignChiDo?

Absolutely! Studies show that language problems in children are associated with stressful pregnancies. SignChiDo is an excellent way to manage stress. The diaphragmatic breathing exercises will not only help with decreasing the levels of stress hormones during pregnancy, but will also strengthen the lungs and diaphragm for delivery.

The two sides of the brain become specialized during fetal development. The right hemisphere grows faster and favors characteristics like emotion. The left hemisphere grows later and develops characteristics such as language. During the fetal developmental period, SignChiDo can be a very effective way of reducing stress while at the same time introducing certain emotions that can affect fetal development in a positive way. Remember, in SignChiDo, we are using words to depict certain emotions that are translated into movement. The circulating neuropeptides that occur when positive emotions are expressed can potentially lay the groundwork for how the brain becomes wired during that fetal developmental period.

Studies show that bad experiences during pregnancy increase the risk of developing a wide variety of illnesses in the child including aggression, language problems, depression, and immune system dysfunction. This confirms the fact that SignChiDo can only benefit the fetus and provide a great method of stress management and relaxation for mothers, while at the same time preparing them for the delivery.

Can Sign Chi Do help with depression?

Yes. There is a great deal of research to suggest that stress leads to depression. It is documented that the body secretes more of the stress-related chemical called cortisol in depressed individuals. That is why it is so important not to suppress emotions. High levels of these stress-related chemicals affect the brain cells by causing them to shrink and sometimes even die. This is evident when comparing the size of certain parts of the brain in people with depression compared to those who are not depressed.

Sign Chi Do was designed to facilitate the flow of your emotions so that they can be expressed in a creative, empowering way through your movements.

What are neuropeptides?

Neuropeptides are chemicals released from the brain in response to certain emotions. Several different neuropeptides have been identified including dopamine, serotonin, glutamate, and endorphins.

Dopamine is important in physical motivation. Being motivated to undertake physical activity is related to this chemical called dopamine.

Serotonin is known as the "feel good" chemical. It has a profound effect on mood and anxiety. High levels of serotonin result in serenity and optimism and can improve sleep.

Glutamate is a chemical that acts as a link between brain cells. This is vital for learning and long-term memory. Mental exercises described in this book tend to strengthen the link between cells, resulting in improved memory.

Endorphins are morphine-like substances found naturally in the body. They promote a sensation of calmness, almost a floating-in-air feeling. The main function of this chemical is that it helps to reduce pain and stress. Relaxation exercises, such as SignChiDo, have been found to increase these endorphin levels, thereby enhancing overall health and wellness.

As a physician, I am convinced that having a basic understanding of how your brain works can only enhance your outlook on life. Understanding why certain emotions occur in response to these chemicals is the first step toward controlling your emotions, instead of allowing them to control you.

References

Moore,Keith L. ed. Clinically Oriented Anatomy, 2nd ed. Williams &Wilkins, 1985.

Gilman, Sid and Newman, Sarah Winans ed. Essentials of Clinical Neuroanatomy and Neurophysiology, 7th Ed. Philadelphia: F.A. Davis Company, 1987.

Kotulak, Ronald ed. Inside the Brain, Revolutionary Discoveries of How the Mind Works, Kansas City: Andrews McMeel Publishing, 1997.

Newberg M.D., Andrew et al, ed. Why God Won't Go Away, New York: Ballantine Books, 2001.

Huang, Alfred ed. Complete Tai-chi, The Definitive Guide to Physical & Emotional Self-improvement. Vermont and Japan: Charles E. Tuttle Company, 1993.

Cohen, Kenneth S. ed. The Way of Qigong. New York: Ballantine Books, 1997.

Sternberg ,Ed.D, Martin L.A. ed. American Sign Language Dictionary, revised edition. 1998.

Fitzgerald M.D. PhD, M.J.T. ed. Neuroanatomy Basic & Applied. Philadelphia: Bailliere Tindall, 1985.

Rama, Swami, Ballentine M.D., Rudolf, Hymes M.D., Alan ed. Science of Breath, A Practical Guide. 3rd ed. Pennsylvania: The Himalayan International Institute of Yoga Science and Philosophy, 1981.

Flodin, Mickey ed. Signing Illustrated. New York: The Berkley Publishing Co. A Perigee Book, 1994.

Hoppenfeld, M.D., Stanley ed. Physical Examination of the Spine and Extremities. Connecticut: Appleton-Century-Crofts, 1976.

A Note From Dr. Anne Borik

When practicing Sign Chi Do it is important to remember that it is an expression of yourself. I designed this basic Sign Chi Do book/DVD in a way that takes you step by step through each word enabling you to design your own fitness phrase.

I want to personally thank you for your interest in Sign Chi Do. I hope that you find it to be a valuable tool that can be used to enhance your physical, mental and spiritual well-being.

UPCOMING:

Advanced Sign Chi Do

Sign Chi Do for Kids

Sign Chi Do in Prayer
(Moving prayer)